Live Growth Focused Young Adult Edition

How to Excel in Life with a Growth Mindset

Dr. Michelle Ihrig

Live Growth Focused Young Adult Edition: How to Excel in Life with a Growth Mindset

Cover designed by Dr. Michelle Ihrig

Special thanks to the following envato elements designers:
aHandDrawn
betoalanis
ddraw
iconbunny
iconsoul
jumsoft
Middtone
and especially: wowomnom

Live Growth Focused
www.LiveGrowthFocused.com

Printed in the United States of America

First Printing: July 2022
Live Growth Focused

ISBN-13 978-1-946568-49-6

This book is dedicated to the
thousands of students
who shaped me into the educator
I am today, and to the
administrators and supervisors
who gave me the freedom to create,
to dream, and to inspire.

Why waste time proving over and over
how great you are,
when you could be getting better?

Why hide deficiencies
instead of overcoming them?

Why look for friends or partners
who will just shore up your self-esteem
instead of ones who will also challenge you to grow?

And why seek out the tried and true,
instead of experiences that will
stretch you?

The passion for stretching yourself
and sticking to it, even (or especially)
when it's not going well,
is the hallmark of the growth mindset.

This is the mindset that allows people
to thrive during some of the most challenging
times in their lives.

—CAROL DWECK

CONTENTS

Introduction

Hi Lovies!

Yes, I am not your teacher, you are 16-22 year-olds, and you are holding a book that you may or may not want to be reading right now. Every time I write one of these books, I picture some students I know who are in the age range and write the book as though I am talking to them.

For this book, the group I am focusing on is my former students who read most of the original teen book three years ago as freshmen and who, like you, see adulthood on the horizon. They will forever be "Lovies" to me, and I will forever be the person who taught them that "sugar shoots" and "fudgsicle" are PG-friendly words to describe mistakes and frustrations.

Regardless if I taught you in the past, just like them, you are unique, valued, talented, and loved. So although our interactions may only be in the confines of this book, please consider thinking of me as your mentor, coach, teacher, Obi-Wan, whatever title makes the most sense to you. I promise you my genuine hope and desire is to inspire you to become your best self in all areas of your lives. When you live growth focused, your entire life could change as well as the lives of those around you.

So, perhaps I'm the cheerleader next to you as you take that once "impossible" assessment, the fan who is screaming for you to go for the goal, or better yet, the one whispering just to put your phone away and focus on your studies. Whatever you need me to be, let me be that person in the confines of this book.

We are in this together, and together, you will see that it is possible to live growth focused.

Let's get the next elephant out of the way: I know, I am expecting you to read (or listen) to a book that at this moment likely has no meaning to you. So why should you spend your time going through this? You could be playing video games, working out, writing a song, drawing anime, completing college applications, working at your part-time job, staring at your homework, or tormenting your sibling?

A valid question...and my response is...because I said so!

CHILL OUT! I'm just kidding.

I wrote this book to be a quick read. Each chapter should take about 10-15 minutes to read, and the reflections and action steps will take 15-30 minutes to write or draw. Granted, some of the action steps could take you longer to implement, and I promise it will be worth it.

So please, unless you are trying to get the latest episode or show in before your friends spoil it with group text after group text: CARE enough about YOU to do this for YOURSELF because YOU want to be a BETTER YOU.

Hopefully, you are holding your own paper copy of the book, so you can take advantage of how awesome it is. Whenever you are bored, start doodling! Yep, I said it; color, draw, write, journal, highlight, etc. If you own it, go at it! We all need brain breaks. I designed this book with lots of blank space for doodles and journaling. There are plenty of images for coloring to give you time to reset your brain and get back to reading, reflecting, and becoming a better you. If this book is yours, make it yours!

Ultimately, it is YOUR decision to have a changed mindset and live growth focused. Someone else may be expecting you to read/journal/draw in the book, but what you do with the knowledge is entirely up to you. My sincerest hope is that you find at least one or two things (hopefully more) which impact you, and as a result, you enjoy a better life.

Warmly,

Doc Chelle

Chapter 1

Because We Grow

In 2006, a researcher named Carol Dweck from Stanford published *Mindset: The New Psychology of Success*. The book was targeted at adults and officially introduced the concept of a GROWTH MINDSET.

In her book, Dweck highlights two types of mindsets: Fixed Mindset vs. Growth Mindset.

When you think of a fixed mindset, I want you to think about getting an "F" on an assignment. Why? Because IT SUCK-A-DOODLE-DOOs!!!

A fixed mindset is all about phrases like....

I can't do this.

I'll never be good at sports.

I failed (again).

I'll never get better.

Why should I try?

My top three schools rejected my application, so much for college.

Pretty much, picture good ol' Eeyore on the gloomiest of days possible...or Grumpy from *Snow White*, Grouchy from *The Smurfs*, Squidward from *Sponge Bob*, Charlie

Brown from...um....*Charlie Brown* or even when Luke Skywalker hid in *Star Wars: The Force Awakens*.

Fixed-minded people look at their circumstances or qualities and believe they have no power to change them.

Who wants to live in a state of doom and gloom? It'd be like playing Fortnite with no ammo or having a cell phone with no service!

Sound the trumpet ringtone!!!

In comes what Dweck calls the "growth mindset." A growth mindset is just the opposite...

I can do this (or even better, WE can do this TOGETHER).

I'll keep working hard, and I'll improve.

My parents' math skills have nothing to do with my ability.

I failed again...ok, great...what can I learn from this.

I got this.

No worries, I know the right school is out there.

A person with a growth mindset looks at situations as opportunities to be UBER amazing!

With a growth mindset, your circumstances or qualities are merely attributes and small pieces of what makes up YOU. There may be days when these elements seem to be your entire existence...but by and large, they are just components.

Instead, who YOU decide to be and the actions YOU take to become that person despite the obstacles far outweigh ANY situation.

One of my students described a fixed mindset as "a kind of poison for the brain" that "makes you believe you will only be good at certain things...that you will never be able to change yourself." On the other hand, my student described having a growth mindset as "like a medicine for the brain" by helping you "to succeed when you try new things" and, best of all, "encourage you to keep trying instead of always quitting."

Lovie, when you truly realize the power YOU possess to shape YOURSELF into the person YOU want to become, YOUR whole world could change. Life is about learning from experiences, and that is the premise of living growth focused.

I HAVE THE POWER TO CHANGE MY LIFE

Reflection Question #1

What is the difference between a fixed mindset and a growth mindset?

Reflection Question #2

In what areas of your life do you already exhibit a growth mindset? How has having a growth mindset in those areas impacted your development or success?

Action Step #1

Start a list of the areas you want to grow in. Then, as you read the book, add to the list and include any other ideas that develop.

Action Step #2

If you are reading an electronic version or are reading your copy of this book, annotate and highlight as you read so you can easily refer to relevant passages. Otherwise, write the page and paragraph numbers as well as the key phrases in a notebook.

Chapter 2

Beware of the Doom and Gloom

Now that we covered the difference between a fixed mindset and a growth mindset, we will explore how maintaining a growth mindset can help us process through some of the most challenging times of our lives. In general, a person with a growth mindset does not allow difficult times to consume them. When something happens, can there be a moment of frustration, of course! Yet, the person reflects on the situation and moves forward after a short period.

In my experience, when challenging situations enter our lives, they occur either because of something we did, something someone else did, or simply for no explainable reason. Of course, there are numerous gray areas where two or more people are involved, a chain of events occurring, etc., but for our purposes, and to keep this section short, let's consider those three possibilities.

Caused by the Growth-Minded Person

Let's first address how growth-minded people react to difficult situations that are mostly, or entirely, their faults. First, the person takes ownership of what happened. Next, they reflect on the occurrence and determine steps to prevent it from happening again. Then, and possibly with the help of others, a plan is created and implemented to get through the situation. Finally, if the person's actions impact other people, a sincere apology is appropriate.

Here is an example. You are at college and agree to hang out with one of your friends on the weekend. A couple of days later, a group from class invites you to join them at the campus hall for movie night. Unfortunately, everything happens so quickly that you forget to follow up with the first friend, and with your phone on silent during the movie, you miss the texts wondering where you are.

So, what do you do? First, when you finally notice your mistake, you contact your friend and apologize. You don't need to go into details about your friendship. Be honest: you forgot, and your actions were inconsiderate.

Next, offer an alternative to connect if they are still open to it, and promise that you will add it to your phone's calendar to make sure you remember. (It may also be generous to offer a coffee, snack, etc., on your outing.)

Lastly, offer your apologies once more, and realize that it is perfectly acceptable for your friend to either accept it or not accept it. If this is your first mistake, forgiveness is on the horizon. However, if this happens frequently, you may need to reflect on your actions more.

I realize the example above is over-simplified; however, I want to emphasize the process. 1) Admit the mistake, 2) Reflect and plan how to prevent it from happening again, 3) Implement a plan to remedy the situation, and 4) Seek forgiveness.

Difficult Situations Caused by Others

Now, if someone else is responsible for causing the situation, the process is similar. First, we acknowledge what happened. In this case, we cannot take ownership of what occurred, nor can we expect the other person to take ownership! I want to make this very clear. A fixed-minded person seeks the apology for vindication to move forward. A growth-minded person moves forward regardless of the deserved apology.

Second, we reflect on how what happened is negatively impacting our lives. Then, with the help of others, we develop and implement steps to work through what occurred. Lastly, we continue our lives being grateful we moved (or are moving) through the situation instead of staying in the "doom and gloom."

For example, in 2020, I was rear-ended as the fifth person in line tried to run a yellow light. Reflecting on the accident a year later, it could have been significantly worse from a bodily injury standpoint. Nonetheless, the person's actions triggered injuries requiring physical therapy and put me in a mental health spiral that took quite some time to break.

Every time I woke up in the middle of the night because of the pain, I would stay up for hours thinking about how she kept me from sleep. Then, every time I went to physical therapy, I spent a few moments utterly livid over her actions and how they impacted my day. Transparently, I could write pages of all the phrases I let circle my mind and prevent me from moving forward.

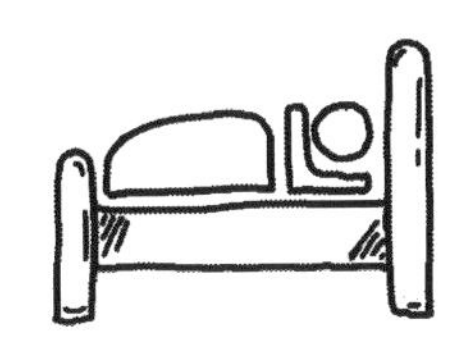

What helped me to get through this situation was the process above. First, I acknowledged I was in a car accident of no fault of my own (I did delete the sugar shoots and fudgicle adjectives I originally typed to describe the driver). Second, I recognized how the situation was negatively impacting me: I allowed a spiral of thoughts to prevent me from living my life to the fullest because of the accident.

Next, through the support of friends, I set actionable goals of things I wanted to accomplish that went to the wayside while I continued to replay the accident and its effects on my life. I also relied on my support network to check in on my progress. Lastly, I remain grateful that the accident, and my reaction to what happened, are no longer central to my life.

Take a few moments to reflect on situations you are dealing with that are caused by someone else. Of course, the challenges you face are yours, and I realize the process above is over-simplified. But, I assure you, I am not trying to diminish what you went through, and depending on the circumstance, you may benefit from professional support. Instead, I am saying that a growth-minded person strives to be future-focused and refuses to allow the actions of others to become stumbling blocks that prevent us from moving forward.

Situations Out of Anyone's Control

Lastly are situations that happen to us out of any one person's control. These are sometimes the most challenging to get through because they can be inexplicable: the loss of a loved one, a global pandemic, the loss of a job, a natural disaster. I do not want to make light of the seriousness of this or any unfavorable situation, and I believe that our mindset can help us persevere through the obstacle.

Years ago, I went on a life adventure to Minnesota. When I applied for a position in student achievement, I had never even been to the state! So when I found out they wanted to interview me, I hopped into my 2009

Nissan Cube named Rubix, and I drove out to Minnesota during Spring Break. Two months later, I was moving to the state.

From my experiences there, I can quickly tell you two COMPLETELY different stories. I will start with the doom and gloom story.

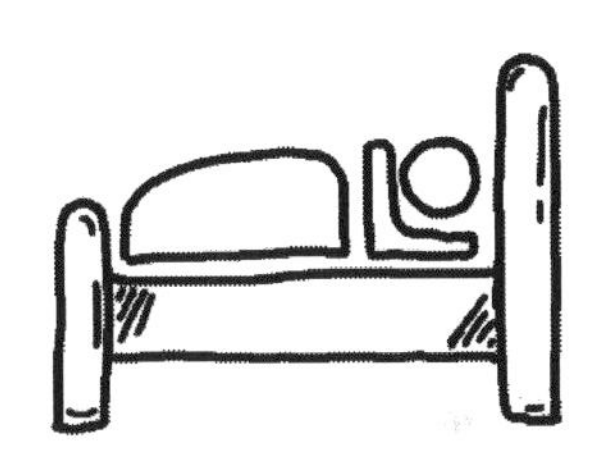

Wanted to live in the same neighborhoods as my students, so I lived in a high-crime area. Heard gunshots coming from the lot next to my property and spent the rest of the night awake in bed in fear. Witnessed a drive-by shooting in a neighboring city and had to call the police as I sped away from the scene. Got into a car accident where I hit a parked car (don't ask).

If I allow my mind and memories to focus on these occurrences in Minnesota, it could appear that it was a horrible experience – which it wasn't.

Here are the memories I choose to share about my time in the land of 10,000 lakes (aka Minnesota).

Lived in a diverse area of the city and got to meet and interact with people from different cultures. Lived within walking distance to a large park and during the summer, walked often and lost weight. Became connected to a family and helped them during a challenging time. Developed a plan to reform a struggling educational program. Grew as a person and learned more about what I can do if I try.

In the first example, I seem like a victim where everything went wrong, yet in the second instance, I sound like an overcomer, better yet a champion!

I share this with you because we ALL have stories...many of you will have stories worse than mine...perhaps with strands of abuse, neglect, poverty, loss...only YOU genuinely know YOUR story...and that's great; because it is YOURS!

and...

Only YOU can share YOUR story in a way that brings light and, better yet, lets YOU shine like the brightest star.

Cue - awe-inspiring ringtone.

The bottom line, Lovie, is YOU are in control of YOU and YOUR destiny. Granted, teachers, parents, coaches, mentors, aunties, etc., definitely have expectations for your life, but how YOU decide to follow those expectations, surpass them, etc., that's entirely your choice.

Please, Lovies, don't allow your circumstances to put you in a place you don't want to be...change your mindset and look at the events to be a better you. As another one of my students stated: "Just because I didn't get it at first doesn't mean I won't get it the fifth time." Life is full of making mistakes. But, true strength comes from learning from our mistakes to be the best we can be.

LEARN=

GROW

Reflection Question #3

Who in your life is living growth focused? Describe what their doom and gloom story could have been and how they are instead living as an overcomer. If you can't think of someone, find a famous person as an example.

Reflection Question #4

Why is it helpful to look forward at what could be rather than what happened in the past?

Action Step #3

Write your own overcomer story. In good writing practice, outline to ensure you cover all the points that matter to you. Then go for it.

Action Step #4

Create an Instagram story, or other visual, of positive memories and moments when you overcame a challenging situation. Then, if you face a future doom and gloom experience, look back to your visual as a reminder you are already an overcomer and the hero of your own story.

Chapter 3

Academics & Careers

Most of you are likely school experts. After ten+ years at school, you know the drill. You realize some people go to school to learn, others to socialize, and others do both. Likely, there are courses you enjoy attending and classes you would rather not take.

If you work, the same is likely valid. Some work for the pay, others work because they enjoy some aspect of the position, and others do both. There are tasks you enjoy doing and tasks that you could easily do without.

Now, more than ever is the time to believe in who you are and to care enough about yourself to make positive steps toward your future. This chapter focuses on being productive whether you are at school, work, part of a club, or even around your house or dorm room.

Previously, many of my students saw changes in their lives when they implemented a growth mindset towards school. For example, one student told me that before having a plan, the homework piled up, and he would "begin to feel overwhelmed and frustrated." Then, he continued, "however, keeping a growth mindset has made school a lot less stressful...when I see a giant pile of papers and assignments...I tell myself if I pace myself, focus, and put forth my best effort, I can do it."

At college, you may feel more alone than ever. Coming up with a plan on how to address your work is vital. In most cases, your professors will give you the due dates for your entire semester's work during the first week. Use a calendar app or physical calendar to write down those dates. Estimate how long each might take you and work backward to determine when you should start the task. Make sure to add time to seek help.

At work or school, there may be tasks that you dislike doing. For me, at work, it is grading make-up work. It can be so tedious. Although I love that my students want to redo their assignments, I dislike what I need to do because of their growth mindset. So how do I handle it?

First, I schedule a time to focus on this task. Then, when the time comes, I do all I can to focus on the activity at hand, free from distractions. I don't know about you, but I love to get distracted when I don't want to do something. So to counter it, I make a conscious effort to address the task without distraction. In most cases, the arduous task takes less time than I imagined, and I can go on to activities I prefer to do.

This buckle-down-and-do-it mindset ties into the next section on tests...even if you are no longer a student, I am sure you can draw comparisons to other areas.

The Dreaded TEST

Many high schools in the United States expect students to take the PSAT, often during the school day. Other schools even require students to attempt the SAT/ACT, sometimes before some students feel prepared for it.

You may be one of the thousands of students who ask yourself, why do I need to take it, why do I need to try?

Well...indulge me as I share my Planet Fitness story with you.

I have a love-hate-love relationship with going to the gym. Usually, I find myself highly motivated, then something happens - like a vacation - and I am off-track again.

In 2016, I started up at Planet Fitness again. Because school started at 7 am, I would get to the gym between 5 am and 5:30 am. One day, I met a talkative woman who started a conversation with me. Now, when I am doing cardio, I have my routine...I like to sweat, and I love to read. When I am in a good book, time passes quickly. When I have my head up looking around, forget it!

So, this woman says to me, "I hate coming to the gym. Let's come together so we can motivate each other." Granted, I was already motivated, but if she needed to see my bedhead hair in the morning to get to the gym, let her.

The next day, I was already on the treadmill, deep in my book, sweating away, and at a pace that breathing is the primary focus. She hopped on the machine next to me...fine...I stopped reading for the polite pleasantries... then she proceeded to set the treadmill to less than two mph! Can you believe it? A gerbil can walk faster than that!

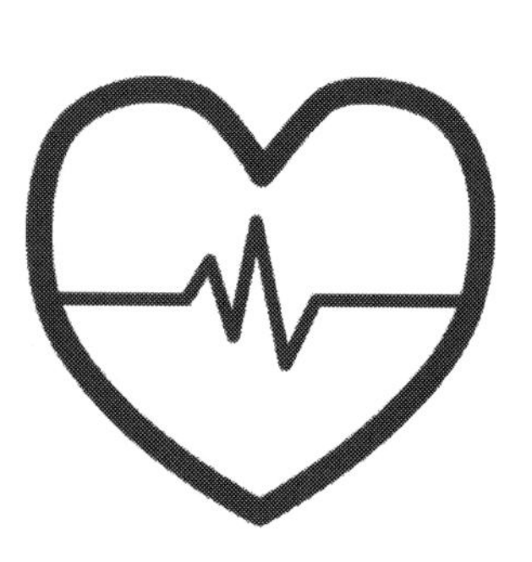

She started to talk to me and not just for me to listen, but to talk back. I was so frustrated!

This woman was not interested in going to Planet Fitness to get healthy; her focus was social.

I couldn't believe it!

Seriously, the HARDEST part of some unwanted but necessary situations is just showing up. Once you are there, you might as well give your best!

The same goes for the SAT, school, a test, or any potentially doom and gloom situation.

I told my students in Connecticut on the morning of the PSAT: "Dude, you are required to sit at your desk for two hours and 45 minutes. No technology, no cell phones, no books, no nothing. A monitor will escort you if you go to the bathroom (who wants that?). The only thing you can do is look at the PSAT in front of you. Since you have to sit at the desk anyway, YOU might as well do YOUR best. The only one you need to impress is YOU!"

I wish you were in the room when they got their results back. So many of my students performed better than they would have dreamed because they CHOSE to do their best.

Years later, my students in Georgia did the same with their state geometry test. We spent the year talking about being your best self, working hard, and seeing results. On test day, they felt confident, stayed focused, and showed up. Weeks later, 92% of my students passed the test, and 64% earned a proficient or distinguished rating. The year before, only 29% of the school's geometry students earned a proficiency or distinguished rating.

I am not saying that if you focus on the test day, you will always do well. I am saying, if you choose to focus and commit to yourself to give your best effort on test day, you will perform better than if you didn't. Furthermore, if you decide to put the time in beforehand, you will likely do even better.

Several years ago, a group of my former students asked me to create an SAT Prep program for them. I was expecting maybe 50 students to sign up. Instead, over 350 students decided to participate. So even with the pandemic going on, we increased our school's mean SAT score by over 70 points.

One of my students experienced significant results in three months. She wrote me, "I want to thank you for all of your review sessions and emphasis on SAT Practice!! This morning I logged in and saw I made 1300 on my March SAT!! This is a 110 point increase from what I made on the December SAT (1190). I'm super excited and extremely happyyy!"

YOUR Choice

Whenever you have something in front of you that you are required/expected to do though might not want to do, you have two options:

1. Work on it between streaming Netflix, looking at your cell phone, and eating Takis...sounds good, right? Well, now, the assignment or project took you longer than it should at a quality less than you are capable of...OR...
2. Care enough about YOU to give YOUR very best and

feel proud of YOURSELF! Turn off the telly, put your phone on silent and AWAY from you (so you're not tempted to look at it), throw in your earbuds (if you need them), and get it done...then feel PROUD of YOURSELF for doing YOUR BEST! Even if you don't get a good grade, who cares? You will know you did your best and now understand what areas you genuinely need help in (instead of the ones you could have gotten correct if you only tried.)

Seriously, I understand the temptation not to perform your best when it is a topic you are not interested in...but instead, with a growth mindset, find ways to make it worth your time.

Have an English essay and hate writing but love programming? Then, look at the assignment to enhance your ability to pay attention to detail because one missing bracket in computer programming can cause detrimental effects to the program's success.

Were you tasked with cleaning the bathroom at your job or dorm room? Yep, I've done it. How did I get through it? Most times played music and just got it done. When I owned my home, my house was always clean. Why? Because it was mine, and I learned how to take care of it when I was younger.

I encourage you, Lovie, when you go to school or work, be your best.

GROWTH= OPPORTUNITY

Reflection Question #5

Consider the Planet Fitness story. When did you not do your best because of your lack of interest or enthusiasm in the task? What was the result of that decision? What upcoming areas in your life can you focus on more?

Reflection Question #6

What are your most significant distractions in life? How do they prevent you from reaching your full potential?

Action Step #5

Imagine your perfect study room or study situation. Make a list of at least five components of your ideal study space. Is it the kitchen table? Your bedroom? With music or without music?

Now, what can you do to arrange your surroundings to resemble your best space? Then, make the necessary changes the next time you have an assignment to complete.

Action Step #6

Think of an upcoming task or assignment that you are not interested in doing. First, reflect on the work. If you put your best effort in, how long would it take you to complete it? What is your deadline? Now, create (and implement) a plan of action to accomplish your task. Then, repeat the process for future tasks.

Chapter 4

Poisonous Drama

Let's face it: life is full of drama, especially when you are a young adult. So it makes sense; this is when you discover who you are and lay the foundation of who you will be in the future.

In high school, I was UBER involved in clubs ranging from cultural groups to student government. From my participation in these organizations, I learned about leadership, service, entrepreneurship, embracing differences, and, quite frankly, the belief that I can change the world - or at least someone else's world - for the better. I was still involved in college, and I added a group of people that I still maintain friendships with... all of the people? No, but a handful, absolutely!

During the pandemic, some of your friendships likely changed. So as you get back to life at school, I encourage you to meet people who will strengthen you and stay away from people who could bring you down.

A few years from now, all the people who caused you to stress will likely be dispersed across the country and world pursuing their specific dreams. No one will care about what one person said to another person because they will be so focused on what lies ahead of them.

Lovies, I encourage you...have the career/college growth mindset now! Instead of worrying about fitting in and being different than who you are to impress someone that in a few years you will likely only see once every five years at the reunion, be the real authentic you, now. Don't be a poser...don't try to be someone you're not just to get a gal or guy to look at you.

Realize that only rarely do relationships that start at this time of your life will continue years later. Please, stop trying to fit in or be someone you are not, you are hindering your ability to be YOUR best YOU, and YOU deserve better than that!

Dealing with Drama

A person with a fixed mindset struggles when it comes to drama. They analyze every look, every comment, and take what is said about them personally. Remember the meme "I'm rubber you're glue," or the classic Pee-Wee line "I know you are, but what am I?"

A person with a fixed mindset takes the negative or neutral comments as actions against them and internalizes those words or actions to form a negative concept of self. Instead of being rubber, the comments stick. Not only do they stick, but they also penetrate the soul.

Now, Lovie, I can't imagine you being the giver of a comment or action that could put someone down, but let's just say that you may be. Perhaps you are not the most vocal person, but you are present.

Here's a fact: research consistently shows that people who hurt others through words or actions are often the recipient of such occurrences from someone else.

For example, people who put others down at school may have an older sibling belittle them at home; or perhaps when they were younger, they were bullied by others and decided when they were older to be the aggressor. Likewise, a person who shuns or ignores someone at school was likely previously shunned or ignored.

The truth is: anyone who consciously puts another person down through action or inaction does not demonstrate a growth mindset. On the contrary, such occurrences are poison to your brain, soul, and future.

PLEASE, I BEG of YOU, CARE enough about YOURSELF to focus on YOU and let the drama fizzle away. YOU and YOUR FUTURE are too important for a "he said, she said" drama battle at work or school. As one of my Lovies shares, "Your growth mindset will allow you to stay positive throughout the argument and be the bigger person when replying." This is not reality TV, *Dr. Phil*, or *Maury*; this is life. So make conscious steps to move away from drama and live growth focused. You don't need poison in your life, and no one else does either.

Reflection Question #7

Does your peer group have drama? Who are the main instigators of the drama? What is going on in their lives which could be a reason for their harmful actions? What can you do to help the person see how their actions impact others and possibly help them shift their ways?

Reflection Question #8

Are you a perpetrator of drama? Even in your friend circle and when you are "just kidding," do you tend to put other people down? Is there a person that annoys you? Do you treat the person differently? How do your actions help or hurt the other person?

Action Step #7

Think about your future. What interests you? Who do you want to be when you grow up? Where do you foresee yourself going to college? What kind of car do you want to drive? What type of home do you want to have? Now, who in your current school or peer circle do you honestly see in your life in the future? Probably few. Make a list of action steps regarding how you can separate yourself from the poisonous drama.

Action Step #8

Spend some time researching meditation, fitness, or prayer if you or your family is spiritual. Then, find some time each day to meditate or reflect and find some level of peace. As you perfect your skill, practice finding peace, even when the chaos of life surrounds you.

Chapter 5

Technology Woes

This section may be the hardest to commit to for some of you, and that's okay. Living growth focused is a process.

Social media, gaming, technology, etc., are parts of our lives.

Back in the Day

When I was your age, we connected to the internet via dial-up through our landline phone line! Ever seen *You've Got Mail* with Meg Ryan and Tom Hanks? Yep, that was how we got online at home. Don't even get me started on how much space my computer at college took up on my dorm desk.

As a student, there were no 1:1 devices and no cell phones! My keyboarding class was ten weeks on a typewriter and ten weeks on a new Mac, which essentially had word processing. It is incredible how much our world has changed in 20 years.

In many ways, life was far less complicated. News to share? We made phone calls! There were no group texts, chats, or social media posts. Mobile phones were essentially car phones attached to boxes in only a few cars, and each minute cost 25 cents. When I worked at a school in the early 2000s, there was massive drama because students circulated a bullying EMAIL...not pics, not group texts, an EMAIL.

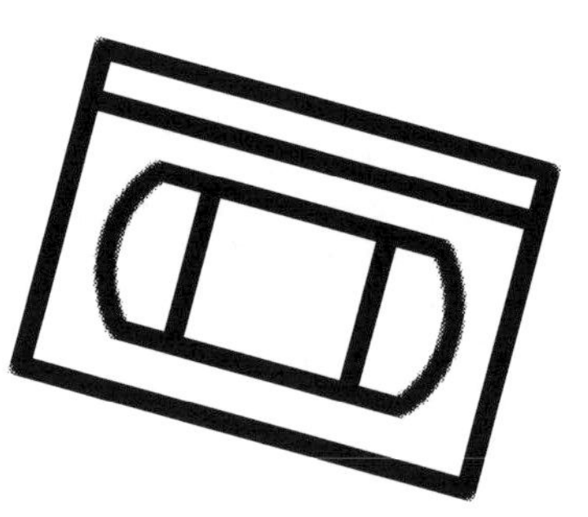

For entertainment, there was no YouTube. We had network (maybe cable) tv, and there was no Netflix - we could rent a movie (a VHS tape) at Blockbuster or borrow one from the library – that's the place in the community with lots of books and resources. So our choices and distractions were, compared to now, limited.

The bottom line is that technology was only a tiny piece of what we did and how we lived. So, we went out, socialized, hung out at the mall, went to the bowling alley, went to the park...you get the idea.

Regarding social relationships, there was drama, there were rumors, there were (sadly) bullies, but it did not consume us. When we went home, for the most part, we were emotionally safe.

Fast Forward

Today, technology has the potential to interfere with our ability to connect and to grow.

In 2016, CNN posted an article titled "Half of Teens Think They're Addicted to Their Smartphones;" Kelly Wallace wrote the article.

The article highlighted the results of a poll of 1200 parents and their teenagers aged 12 to 18 for Common Sense Media. Common Sense is a non-profit focused on helping stakeholders, in essence, you, parents, schools, and policymakers, to understand the effects of media and technology.

One of the alarming statistics referenced in the article is that 59% of teens say they are addicted to technology. Regarding parents, 66% of parents feel their teens spend too much time on mobile devices, and of that, 52% of the teenagers surveyed agreed. People are so addicted to their cell phones that 69% of parents and approximately 77% of teenagers check their devices at least hourly.

59%

Here is an example of one of the struggles that I overcame. In early 2017, I became obsessed with the game Ramsay Dash. Chef Gordon Ramsay is an avatar and a culinary mentor; as the player cooks digital recipes and serves endless customers, avatar Ramsay monitors. Ramsay either told me I was brilliant or a %@*% at the end of each level.

I became obsessed with achieving three stars on every level that I spent well over 1-2 hours a day playing the game. Not in one sitting, but 10 minutes here, 15 minutes there, you get the picture. I encouraged myself by saying playing the game was good for the brain. The reality is, I could have done so many other things with the hours upon hours that I spent playing Ramsay Dash. In one week alone, I spent nearly 10 hours playing a game on my phone...added together that's one extra day I could have done something productive with my life.

Another example that I am not entirely proud of is my occasional addiction to Netflix. My obsession doesn't last long, but when I get a series that I am very interested in (aka *Stranger Things*), I comfortably sit on my couch and stream episode after episode after episode. I'm sure you have no idea what I'm talking about :-).

Lovies, stop spending hours on Snapchat, Instagram, TikTok, or other social media, especially at school or work. Stop playing Fortnite, Minecraft, Roblox, or any other gaming station for long sessions at a time. Please turn it off or silence it, and take a break. You deserve peace.

The Google Way

In an article published in Wired magazine entitled "How Googlers Avoid Burnout (and Secretly Boost Creativity)," authors Stulberg and Magness outline a program started at Google over ten years ago to help Googlers (aka Google employees) unplug. Early Googler Chade-Meng Tan developed a seven-week course on meditation and mindfulness. The program was so successful that five years later, the program became a non-profit organization to help people around the globe to unplug. As a result, over 20,000 people in over 200 cities have learned the power of disconnecting.

The research backs up the benefits of stepping away, too! Instead of sitting at your computer and going back and forth between devices, especially when you are stuck on a problem or project, take a break by going for a walk or run, doing yoga, getting a snack, or even taking a shower. Research suggests that as much as 40% of all your creative ideas occur when you are not trying to have them. When you actively think about a topic, it is called deliberate thought, but almost half of great ideas happen when you are not trying to have them!

To achieve the success that you truly deserve, you must care enough about yourself to unplug. I'm not asking you to turn everything off forever, but love yourself enough to know that you can be so much more if you decrease your use of devices.

LOVE YOURSELF!

Reflection Question #9

Consider your use of technology. Truthfully, how many times a day do you check your phone...in class, at home, while doing your homework? How has your use of technology helped or hindered your overall success?

Reflection Question #10

What aspects of technology are your pitfalls? Are you glued to Netflix, Fortnite, or social media? When are you most likely to turn on your device? When you are bored? Is it when you have a task in front of you that you don't want to do?

Action Step #9

Make a list of everything you may have missed out on because of your tendency to choose technology over other tasks. For example, how have your relationships with others been impacted? How could future possibilities be affected if you continue to use technology at your current level?

Action Step #10

Create several small goals for yourself to limit the amount of technology you use. Please do not limit the technology you need for school, work or some other positive experience, like writing a book or creating a YouTube channel. Once you develop your goals, start implementing the goals, and take actionable steps to disconnect from technology and connect with life.

Chapter 6

Working Together

You likely worked with others, perhaps as a member of an athletic or academic team or during a collaborative task at school or work. Working with others helps us develop our soft skills, such as communication, collaboration, and fair play.

Joining a team or group can offer you the encouragement that you need to shine and be your best you. There will be people to bounce ideas off and learn from, and you can be a source of help and support for the others on your team. Teams can be as small as you and one other person or a large group of people.

One of my students wrote, "In Sports, my growth mindset is to get better every day. To do that, I will need to be able to challenge myself and overcome some limits....Not only do I try and become a better player but also work on being the best teammate I can be, by showing up to all the practices and trying my hardest every practice, not just for myself but also for my teammates."

Most of us can share some dreary examples of teamwork. I recently led this chapter with a group of 8th graders, and the comments they shared about teams shocked me because many of the challenges they faced are the same they could experience as adults. We talked about how every group usually has a mixture of some the following:

- People who want to be the leader and may compete for the role
- People who speak frequently, and sometimes over others
- People who take the ideas of others as their own without providing fair credit
- People who just don't seem to care and do nothing
- People who do most of the work (not always the leader) so that it gets done

Patrick Lencioni wrote *The Five Dysfunctions of a Team* and sold over three million copies of his book. I will not go through all of his book; however, I want to highlight some key concepts.

First, the foundation of a good team is <u>trust</u>. Specifically, teammates need to respect each other. So how do we do this? First, we get to know each other. Then, we are respectful of our strengths and areas of growth.

Next, good teams embrace positive conflict. Instead of just one person's idea, everyone shares and has a voice, even if people disagree. Once all ideas are discussed, the team makes a collective decision to move forward.

Third, the team commits to the idea and to the steps needed to accomplish the collective goal. Each member completes the assigned tasks and supports the other members if help is needed.

Fourth, team members hold each other accountable. For example, if one person appears to be struggling with follow-through, the team inquires about the reasons and supports as needed. Lastly, the team's focus is on the overall team's success, not each member's contribution.

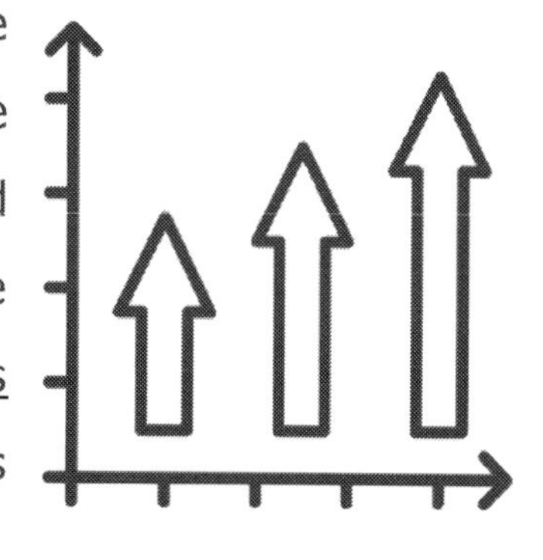

Now we will consider how Lencioni's work can relate to your experiences at work or school. For example, perhaps you work at a retail shop. Likely, you are not a manager yet; however, you can positively impact your store.

First, get to know the other people who work at the store. You don't need to spend hours talking with them, but learn who they are. Are they students like you, have families, or have multiple jobs to coordinate? What are their interests? What makes them happy? Knowing little pieces of information like this can build trust. Specifically, when a team member asks you to take their shift because their child is sick, understanding their story may give you more compassion. If there is a teammate who excels at organizing, learning from them will only make you better.

Next, good teams have good conflict. Again, I am not suggesting pitching an argument just to insight conflict; however, if you have an idea that can benefit your store, you should share it! You can start by bringing the idea to your immediate supervisor. See what the person says, ask to try it out. If the person disagrees with your idea, that's fine! Please write it down because, who knows, you might get to implement it later. Also, do NOT talk badly about the person or try to gain the support of others once your leader says no; that could only make things worse.

Third, be a good teammate. Show up to work early, instead of on time. When you arrive a little early, you can get your stuff together so you can start work on time. You might need to leave home earlier, just to allow for unexpected delays. I live in a city of over 6 million people! My commute to work can take 15 minutes, or it can take me 45 minutes to an hour if there is an accident. Leaving earlier is critical to my commitment to be ready to work on time.

Fourth, follow through with your work tasks, even if it is a task that you do not like. Also, if you see a teammate struggling, offer to help if you are able. We don't want it to become a pattern, yet we all experienced moments when an extra hand makes things so much easier.

Lastly, it is easy to look at a job as a paycheck, especially entry-level jobs. When we look at work in that way, it becomes more like work. Instead, when we look at it as a place where we can contribute to our success, the success of our teammates, and the success of the store, then it becomes more meaningful and less laborious.

When it comes to being part of a team at school, we can follow the same tenets and achieve success. First, we get to know our teammates. What strengths can we bring to the team? Next, we openly discuss our assignment and share ideas so that everyone has a voice. Third, we stick to the agreed plan, and we work to meet our deadlines. Fourth, if someone seems to be struggling, we understand why, and we offer support. Lastly, we maintain our focus on the end goal: a completed, high-quality assignment.

Having a growth mindset while working with others will make your life infinitely better...and it makes life's challenges more comfortable to accept. There will be challenges...and that is a-okay...because when we live growth focused, we learn from our trials.

WE MUST LEARN ABOUT EACH OTHER: OUR STRENGTHS AND AREAS FOR GROWTH ARE JUST THE BEGINNING.

Reflection Question #11

What teams are you part of? The teams could be organized, like in athletics or afterschool clubs, a group of people who share the same interest, or even at your job. If you are not part of a team, what do you enjoy doing, and whom can you connect with to share your passion?

Reflection Question #12

What is the dynamic of your team? For example, are you supportive of each other, or do you tend to put each other down? How do the team dynamics impact the overall success of the team?

Action Step #11

If you are not part of a team or an organization at school, begin to research what activities are available to you. Then, make a list of at least three possible groups and their meeting times. Finally, choose and then visit at least one of your identified groups.

Action Step #12

Consider the dynamics of your team. Make a list of at least seven areas your team can improve...if appropriate, ask a teammate or your whole team to give you ideas. Then create a plan to improve in at least one area. Once you have strengthened that focus, switch to another area of growth.

Chapter 7

Working with Authority

In the younger versions of this book, this chapter focuses predominantly on the relationship between young people and adults, specifically parents and teachers. I briefly considered maintaining that theme; however, I decided to reshape the narrative as you are very close to adulthood. My goal is to equip you with the skills you need to advocate for yourself, at home, at school, and work.

First, life at this stage can be overwhelming. If you are still in high school, you are juggling academics, jobs, college applications, tests, and supporting your family. If you are in college, your workload likely increased dramatically, plus you might be balancing academics, social life, and other commitments. Finally, if you are full-time in the workforce, you probably have financial obligations that may impact your time.

The reality is, the stresses you are experiencing now are worlds different than those many adults faced when we were your age. So how do young adults and adults work together with a growth mindset?

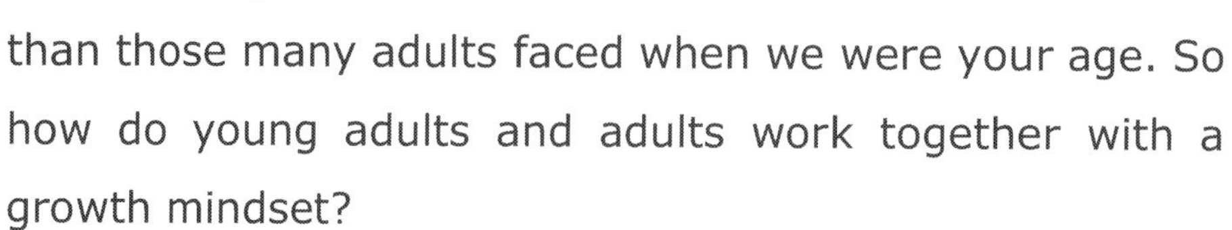

First, we strive to understand each other. We do this by first making a point to find time to talk. With your folks, an argument is NOT the time to talk. With your teachers or professors, during class is not the right time. When your boss is in the middle of an important task is also not a good time.

For example, let's say that you want to attend college out-of-state, (as a side note, I do not recommend doing that unless your scholarships -not loans- are incredible). However, your parents want you to stay at home. So how do you bring up the topic? First, you make a list of the reasons why going to that particular school is essential to you, including information such as cost, scholarships, connection to future careers, and your expectations from your parents.

Then, you give your folks notice that you want to talk. For example, I've been thinking a lot about attending such-and-such university. When would be a good time for us to talk about what I put together?

If you want to talk with your professor or teacher, the method remains the same for this stage: Dear Dr. Ihrig. This is * from your MWF 10:10 am Intro to Sociology class. I am seeking assistance with the reflection paper due in three weeks. When would be a good time to meet?

By following this method, two things happen. First, you

give your folks or professor a heads up about the topic/area of concern. Second, you provide them with a measure of power by letting them pick the time.

When the time comes to meet, please come prepared. In the example with your parents, come with your list. Bring visuals, show them that you care about the topic. If it is the meeting with the professor, print out the assignment. Make notes on it, and prove that you read the task. As an educator, I get frustrated when students ask me questions, such as what chapter we are doing, when I already have it posted on the board and they just didn't read it.

As you meet with the adult, ask for feedback and direction. Keep your emotions in check. This is not the time to burn bridges. Will the adult agree with you even if you put all this time into the discussion? Possibly, possibly not. Some relationships may be slightly worn or ripped... like a pair of your favorite jeans...and if you start the process, I am confident others will notice.

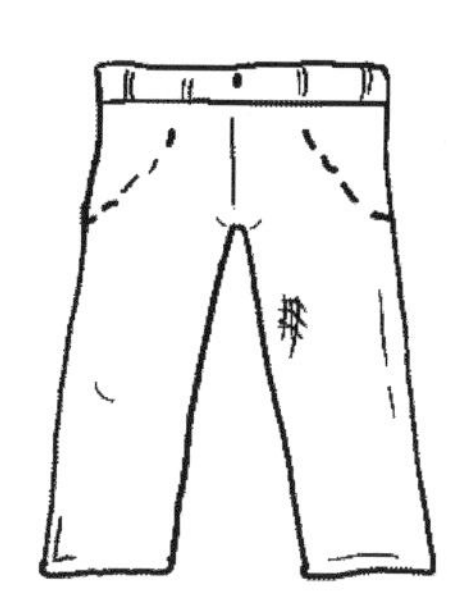

Here is a story, in her own words, from one of my students:

Recently I was wanting to have a stronger relationship with my family. I used to be so close to my parents, we would do so many things together. But as time and life went on, I found myself so careless about them and life. I would start to argue a lot with them.

And I've noticed that I would argue with them over the stupidest reasons like to clean my room or normal house chores. My parents would come home from work, and they would want the house clean. Yet, that was something I didn't give them.

I started to notice that my parents were right and that they do so much towards me and my sister. That the last thing I could do is clean the house and do some extra things for them. So that's what I started to do. When I got home, I would do my homework and get straight into the plan. As days went by, they noticed that this wasn't just a one-time thing. In those days, I noticed that I wasn't arguing as much as I was before. I was not the same lazy person as before, and I wasn't going to get back in the habit. I grew as a person, a daughter, and a sister, and not only did I see my growth, so did others.

Remember, adults, by and large, do want to help you. It just occasionally becomes problematic when we don't understand you.

The Karate Kid

Recently I watched *The Karate Kid* again...not the original 1984 version starring Ralph Macchio and Noriyuki "Pat" Morito as Mr. Miyagi...it was the 2010 version starring Jaden Smith as Dre, Jackie Chan as Mr. Han, and Taraji P. Henson as Dre's mom. The film begins with Dre and his mom leaving Detroit to move to China.

Within the first 15 minutes, Dre begins to experience what sadly plagues many new students, bullying. Unfortunately, instead of opening up to his mom about the harassment and the fears that he is facing, Dre internalizes everything. He even pretended to sleep when she came home to avoid a conversation. However, Dre does tell his mom on one occasion – while screaming in the street – that he hates it in China but again does not explain why.

The issue becomes Dre's lack of willingness to calmly share what he is experiencing, as well as, perhaps, Mom's inability to notice that something is seriously wrong. Thankfully, Dre finds a mentor in Mr. Han and learns Kung Fu to compete against the bully.

The point is this: you are not the only person who has a challenging relationship with a parent, teacher, coach, or another adult. Sadly, it is a phenomenon that many young adults face. If you are willing to take some small baby steps, as my student did above, the relationship will likely end up strengthening. However, if you feel like that relationship is too far broken, and without help it might be, then perhaps following in the footsteps of Smith's character in *The Karate Kid* and finding a mentor may be a viable option.

The bottom line is, we all need people to help us on our journey... people who experienced more than we have, people who may know a bit more, and people who can help us become our best.

WE ALL NEED PEOPLE TO HELP US ON OUR JOURNEYS

Reflection Question #13

Whom in your life do you struggle to communicate with? What are some of the possible reasons why communication is a challenge? What can you do to strengthen the connection between each other?

Reflection Question #14

Which adults in your life do you trust? Who can you go and talk to if you need help? When are the adults available for you? Is there something you have been wanting to talk about but have ignored? How does talking to your trusted adult help you on the path of life?

Action Step #13

If you do not have a trusted adult to speak to, make a list of potential candidates. For example, you may already have a person who understands young adult issues, and perhaps you could benefit from a mentor who could help you in another area of your life, such as preparing for your first job. After you have your list of candidates, pick at least two adults you can connect with, then set up a time to meet them and ask if they could be a mentor to you.

Action Step #14

What adult relationship do you struggle with the most? What actions on your end impact the success of this relationship? Make a list of at least five things you could do to strengthen the relationship with this adult, then take them!

Chapter 8

Discovering Who You Are

Let's face it: high school can be challenging. You have responsibilities and expectations, including homework, clubs and organizations, perhaps a part-time job, and even potentially watching younger members of your family. On top of all those responsibilities, you are at the stage of your life where you discover who you are.

Years ago, a psychologist named Erikson described eight stages that people progress through as they age. The stage that you are in right now is called Identity vs. Role Confusion. Basically, Erikson believed the prominent focus during adolescence would not necessarily be on academics, as it may have been in elementary and middle school, nor would it be on building lasting relationships as it will be in adulthood. Instead, the focus of the teenage (and early young adulthood) years is discovering who you are.

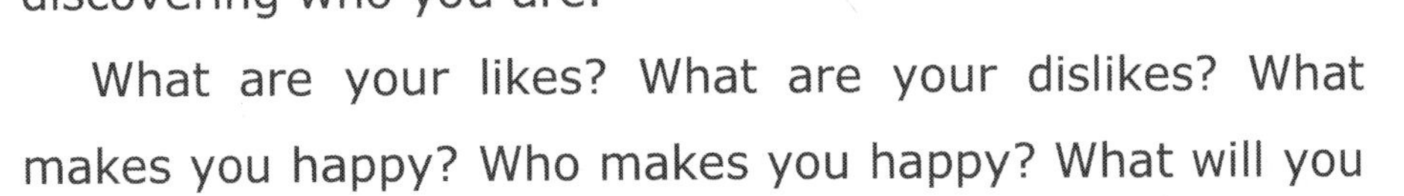

What are your likes? What are your dislikes? What makes you happy? Who makes you happy? What will you do when you graduate (not what do your parents want you to do)? How do you connect with others?

Erikson believed that a teenager would face many conflicts to help shape the individual into who they would become. Here is an example of conflict...you have homework to do, and your friends want to go out. Do you stay home and work, or do you go out? You do well in math and are interested in joining the math league; however, you also love drama and the schedules conflict... which do you choose?

There is an internship available at a local newspaper or even a radio station, and it will take hours of your life to apply for the position and even more hours interning for free. So do you give up your other interests to apply for the internship, and if you get it, do you give up your free time?

You are part of a group of people who make poor choices. You don't want to be part of the group; however, you want to be accepted. Do you follow along with the group, or do you leave the group?

Flashback to the 1980s

One classic example of discovering who you are can be seen in the 1986 cult movie *Pretty in Pink* starring Molly Ringwald as Andie, a girl from the other side of the tracks living with her drunken, single father. Andie is exclusively her own; she makes her own fashion-forward clothes, has a best friend named Duckie (played by Jon Cryer), and is a non-conformist.

In the first 15 minutes of the movie, Andie meets Blane, a wealthy teen from the "A crowd." The entire film focuses on Blane's desire for Andie to adapt, Andie's passion for being who she is, and Duckie's hidden love for Andie. Despite being picked on mercilessly, Andie stays true to herself.

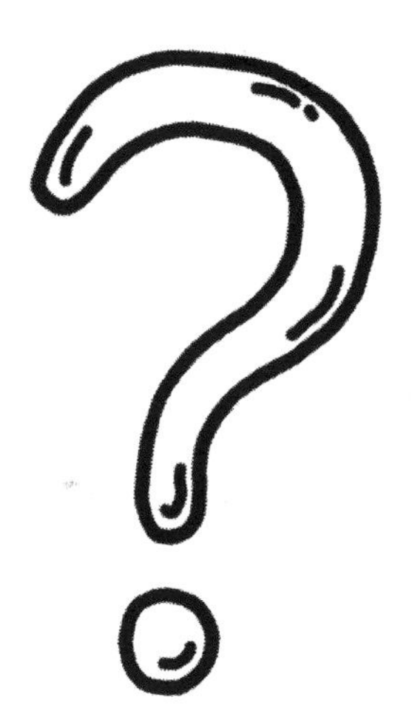

Now I am not suggesting that you buy a sewing machine, collect old clothes from friends, and design your own clothing line; I suggest that you discover who you are, what makes you tick, and what makes you happy. Take personality tests, unplug your TV, put your phone on airplane mode, and just think: Who is the person I want to be? What do I need to do to become that person? Who do I need to help me?

Be Super

Over Spring Break 2018, I confess to binge-watching the first season of *Supergirl*, a CW hit that launched in 2015. The story focuses on Kara Danvers (played by

Melissa Benoist), who is Superman's older cousin on Krypton (though technically is younger than him on earth). The first episode introduces Kara's conflict of either hiding her superpowers or forgoing secrecy and shining. As the series is in its fourth season, I expect you know which avenue she chose.

One of the reasons why Supergirl was so successful is that soon into discovering who she wanted to be she enlisted the support of others. First came James Olsen (played by Mehcad Brooks), who knew her secret already and is a close friend of Clark Kent, aka Superman; James Olsen shared things with her that James learned while working with Superman.

Next, she told her secret to her best friend, Winn Schott (played by Jeremy Jordan), a tech-genius; it is his knowledge that soon assists Supergirl in finding missions, and he also becomes her biggest supporter. Additionally, Supergirl recruits her sister, Alex Danvers (played by Chyler Leigh), and Alex's boss, Director Hank Henshaw (played by David Harewood), to be part of her support network. Because Supergirl's parents died on Krypton, media mogul Cat Grant (played by Calista Flockhart) steps into the role.

The purpose of sharing all this character backstory is simple: even Supergirl needs help. Okay, it is cheesy, I agree, but once you are on the track of discovering who you are and then, more importantly, becoming that person, you will need people to have your back. People who will be your cheerleaders. People who will encourage you...and even people who will suggest you step back and rethink.

Yes, it is possible to grow alone...it is possible to have a growth mindset without the help and the support of others...but do you want to? Lovie, find someone you can trust, a mentor, a friend, even a parent. Share a piece of who you are. Could it backfire? Yes. Could it lift you to a higher level? Definitely, yes!

EVEN SUPERGIRL NEEDS SUPPORT TO TRULY SOAR

Reflection Question #15

Who are you? What makes you happy? What makes you angry? What career would you like to pursue in the future? What actions are you taking right now which can increase your success in this area?

Reflection Question #16

Who in your life is your team of superhero sidekicks helping you achieve your fullest potential? How do they help you? Who else do you need to add to your team?

Action Step #15

If you feel like you don't quite know the real you yet, go online and take a few surveys. These could be career interest surveys, exploring the college board site for the types of colleges you may be interested in, or even completing an online Meyers-Briggs personality survey. Remember, the results will be from an online survey and not the quality you would get in a doctor's office; however, they should give you some ideas to further reflect on.

Action Step #16

Make a list of your best qualities, specifically your attributes that make you feel pride. For example, are you kind, giving, or honest? What hinders your ability to display your best qualities? What qualities do you need or want to improve? Now, make a list of what you can do to improve, then implement at least one of them.

Chapter 9

Be True to You

Challenges, pressures, peers, social media, parents, teachers, friends, ex-friends, and so many more people and things begin to take a more significant role in your life once you move into young adulthood. It can be overwhelming. Thankfully, once you truly embrace a growth mindset, you will be able to separate the challenges into ones that strengthen you, are toxic to you, and those that fall in between.

As we already discussed, this is a challenging time. You don't need to read about it because you already know it! Sometimes, the situations you experience will strengthen you – intellectually, emotionally, or physically. These are the opportunities that you want to embrace, push forward through, and make priorities because they are likely the opportunities that will positively impact your future and potentially the lives of others.

Here is an example. During summer vacation a few years ago, I was surprised to see a former student hanging outside the school. I asked what he was doing; he replied that he was training to be part of the marching band. When I asked him if he enjoyed doing it, his face lit up. I could tell it was a passion for him. Eight weeks later, at the faculty pep rally, I was very proud to see my former student standing in front of everyone else with a long baton – he earned the drum major position!

This student decided he would use his summer for good and become his very best in an area he was deeply passionate about. Maybe marching band isn't for you; perhaps it's athletics, drama, technology, writing, the list goes on. Part of being true to you is to prioritize, as much as possible, what you are passionate about.

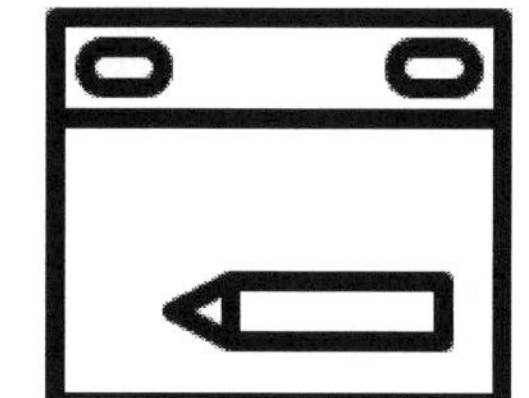

Another student wrote: "I have used growth mindset in my life by trying to become a better artist in both drawing and painting. I pushed myself and made a routine of drawing almost every day to work on my technique, and I just recently became satisfied with my artwork. I felt accomplished and empowered. Someone who just naturally had drawing talent may not appreciate the artwork they made as much as I appreciate my work because they didn't exactly work as hard towards it because art came easier for them in a way." This student put her passion before the thoughts and comments of others. Despite what others thought of her work, she was proud of her accomplishment as she was developing her talent.

Unfortunately, not every situation you experience will be favorable. Some will be toxic, while others will require your reflection on the matter. People, even friends and family, will say or do things to you that are hurtful. Sometimes the words or actions are intentionally cruel, sometimes their intention was humor, and sometimes the person did not even realize their words were harmful.

Lovies, it is not your responsibility to determine the motivation behind the words or actions spoken to you. Still, it IS your responsibility to decide HOW you will let those words or actions impact your moment, day, week, year, and life. That is YOUR decision.

In October 2018, Nadia Murad was one of two people awarded the Nobel Peace Prize; Dr. Denis Mukwege, a surgeon, was the second. In 2014, ISIS terrorists overran Murad's village in northern Iraq. Thousands of women and children from her heritage, the Yazidi minority, were captured, raped, and sold into sexual slavery. Instead of hiding as many of the survivors did after their escape, Murad demanded to be photographed and named. Her advocacy led to the United Nations officially recognizing the genocide of the Yazidi minority at the hands of ISIS terrorists.

The atrocities that Murad, and thousands like her, experienced are unimaginable. Yet, despite the cruelties she faced, Murad would not let that be the end of her story. Instead, she used the situation to empower her.

I encourage you, Lovies. No matter what has happened to you or will happen to you, use your inner strength not to allow the situation to hinder the inner you. YOU ARE TOO VALUABLE, TOO IMPORTANT, and TOO EXCEPTIONAL for your future to be dictated by the hurts of your past.

YOU are an OVERCOMER. YOU

can get through this. Stand up for YOURSELF; get help from a trusted friend or mentor. You MUST be true to yourself...not to what other people's actions could do to you. Living growth focused means you accept what happened, and then you immediately look at how you can grow from the situation and write your own story.

YOU ARE TOO IMPORTANT TO HAVE THE POISON OF YOUR PAST DICTATE YOUR FUTURE

Reflection Question #17

What makes you special and unique? Are these qualities you possessed your entire life, or are they qualities that you developed over time?

Reflection Question #18

What qualities are you not so proud of in your life? What conditions hinder your ultimate growth and success?

Action Step #17

Speak with people who care about you and who you trust. Ask them what they think your best qualities are, and be open enough to ask them what areas they think you could improve in.

Action Step #18

What has been toxic to your success? Next, write or draw how that event impacted you and how it hindered your growth. Now, write about how you will overcome that situation, remembering that an adverse incident does not define you; it strengthens you.

Chapter 10

Laying a Foundation for the Future

Over the past nine chapters, you learned how to implement a growth mindset at school, with friends, and while using technology. Then, we talked about how a growth mindset can help on teams and at home. The last two chapters helped you to think about who you are as a person and the importance of standing up for yourself.

In this final chapter, we will discuss growth mindset and your heart. Knowing the importance of being your best you in all areas of your life will mean little if your heart is not in the right place.

Laying a foundation for the future is about determining a set of values, expectations for yourself, or fundamentals that you will hold in your heart to be not only the best person for you, but also the best person in the lives of others.

The following are key components of my foundation:

• Every person can do good and bring joy to others. Whether they choose to exude happiness is out of my control; however, I can make the conscious decision to bring joy.

• Integrity matters – there is power in words and actions, and living an honest life is achievable.

• Life is a process – I don't have all the answers, and that is okay. What I think or know today could be different tomorrow based on new information and experiences, and that is okay too.

• Asking for help is critical for growth. My best growth comes when I ask for input from others and then make the best decision for me.

• Making mistakes is okay and will happen; it is a natural part of growing. When I make a mistake, I need to learn from it. If my mistake impacted others, I need to own it, so we can all move on.

• Forgiveness, while occasionally painful, is a necessity.

• Parents and caregivers should be respected, despite when I think they may not deserve it or how challenging it may be for me.

• We are interdependent, and we need each other – even when it is hard to admit.

There is so much more that can be expressed about the importance of laying a foundation for the future. Please, spend time over the next pages, seek advice from friends and grown-ups, and just start writing. You can always change or adapt your list later.

INTEGRITY MATTERS: LIVING AN HONEST LIFE IS ACHIEVABLE

Reflection Question #19

What are your core principles, and how do they impact your life?

Reflection Question #20

Who or what influences your principles? Who should you connect with to help you consistently stand on your future foundation?

Action Step #19

Make a list of ways that you could strengthen your foundational values. Then act on your list.

Action Step #20

Write down your foundation in a place you can access easily. If you are comfortable to do so, talk to your parents, your friends, or your teachers about the foundational values you want to follow. Then, when times get tough, revisit your foundation and remember you are not alone. People are willing to help you on your journey.

Chapter 11

The Great Beyond

Congratulations! You almost read the entire book! Woohoo!

Let's take a step back and review the major themes we covered. First, possessing a growth mindset is good...think Growth = Good...If we were in my classroom right now, you would hear me emphasize the G sound; however, that sound is impossible to type. A growth-focused person looks at circumstances as opportunities to learn and to grow. The opposite of the growth mindset is a fixed mindset. People with a fixed mindset are stuck and believe that their circumstances are out of their control.

Then came thoughts on writing our own story. Whatever may have happened in our lives, we can write a story that is doom and gloom or one that makes us the hero of our own story. So, for a happier life, be a hero!

Regarding school, we discussed the importance of planning, seeking help, and pushing ourselves to learn. High school and college is temporary, and drama that happened today will likely be forgotten tomorrow, next week, and indeed years from now. Why let it bother us if it doesn't honestly matter in the scheme of the world? We also learned that people who hurt others verbally or physically were likely hurt themselves.

Next, we learned that technology has changed over the years, and as such, so has the pressures you face. Parents and teens harbor some addiction to technology, so both need to unplug. Even Google teaches their staff to put tech away because creativity often happens when you least expect it.

We discussed the value of participating on a team. Teams can include sports, music, drama, tech, etc. We learn intangible skills like communication, collaboration, and teamwork. We also looked at the importance of bettering ourselves for the good of the team.

Next, we discussed adults...Parents, teachers, coaches, and mentors can seem so one-sided and may, at times, appear not to listen or care. We talked about the *Karate Kid* movie featuring Jaden Smith in which his character moves to China. Although it would have been better to have a conversation with his mother about his concerns, his character sought a mentor to help him navigate the transition.

In Discovering Who You Are, we talked about how in psychology, during the teen years, you are likely more concerned about your peers than your parents as you discover your identity. We focused on the importance of staying true to yourself, not caving into peer pressure, and building a team of people around you to help you reach your highest potential, like Supergirl.

For Be True to You, we revisited the idea of the doom and gloom story and reflected on the importance of following your passions. We also looked at the value of being an overcomer even in the direst of circumstances. Lastly, we discussed the importance of laying a foundation for the future.

So...now what? Now it's time to put a plan in place for you to Live Growth Focused.

Unless you are uber brave, I recommend starting small and gradually adding other areas to improve. For example, perhaps your relationship at home is toxic with your parents. So, spend some time thinking about that relationship, maybe even talking to your folks, and think of some concrete actions you can do to grow that relationship.

Maybe you are in a peer group that is pressuring you to be a person you are not interested in being, but you struggle because you want to be accepted. So, take some time to reflect on the benefits of those relationships and the struggles of those relationships. Write them down to compare. Then decide if the bonds should be mended or if it is time to find a different peer group. Remember, in four years, when everyone is working, or in college, not much of the relationships in high school will matter anyway.

Perhaps your grades are not what you want them to be. Focus on one or two classes first that need the most support. Make appointments with your teachers before or after school (not during class). Come up with a plan to improve...and turn off technology while you're doing your homework! Once the one or two courses are on track, then work on the other ones.

Lovies, the power to Live Growth Focused is in your hands. Not mine, not your parents', not your peers', and not your teachers' hands. YOU need to decide if YOU love YOURSELF enough to be the best YOU that YOU can be, and I believe when you get your act together, YOU will be able to change your world.

I believe in YOU.

With love,
Doc Chelle

Area #1 Action Plan

Where do you want to strengthen your growth mindset?

What is your goal?

What three steps can you take to improve in this area?

Whom can you ask to help you improve?

Area #2 Action Plan

Where do you want to strengthen your growth mindset?

What is your goal?

What three steps can you take to improve in this area?

Whom can you ask to help you improve?

Area #3 Action Plan

Where do you want to strengthen your growth mindset?

What is your goal?

What three steps can you take to improve in this area?

Whom can you ask to help you improve?

Area #4 Action Plan

Where do you want to strengthen your growth mindset?

What is your goal?

What three steps can you take to improve in this area?

Whom can you ask to help you improve?

Doodle Pages

Doodle Pages

Doodle Pages

Doodle Pages

Doodle Pages

About the Author

Dr. Michelle Ihrig is an author/educator based in Atlanta, Georgia. Her gift is the ability to see the greatness in people and to provide them with the tools, resources, and motivation needed to strategically work and to truly shine.

Dr. Ihrig is a certified educator in Mathematics, Special Education, English as an Additional Language, Gifted Education, Online Education, and Administration. Her doctoral focus was best practices of inclusive education at international schools.

Dr. Ihrig is also the author of Scripture Life Devotionals and Black Bear Coloring Literacy Books.

Made in the USA
Columbia, SC
08 July 2022